Heroes for Young Readers

Written by Renee Taft Meloche
Illustrated by Bryan Pollard

Adoniram Judson
Amy Carmichael
Betty Greene
Cameron Townsend
Corrie ten Boom
David Livingstone
Eric Liddell
George Müller

Gladys Aylward
Hudson Taylor
Jim Elliot
Jonathan Goforth
Lottie Moon
Mary Slessor
Nate Saint
William Carey

Heroes of History for Young Readers

Written by Renee Taft Meloche
Illustrated by Bryan Pollard

Clara Barton
George Washington
George Washington Carver
Meriwether Lewis

...and more coming soon

Heroes for Young Readers Activity Guides and audio CDs
are now available! See the back of this book for more information.

For a free catalog of books and materials contact
YWAM Publishing, P.O. Box 55787, Seattle, WA 98155
1-800-922-2143, www.ywampublishing.com

HEROES OF HISTORY FOR YOUNG READERS

GEORGE WASHINGTON CARVER

America's Scientist

Written by Renee Taft Meloche
Illustrated by Bryan Pollard

Emerald Books

P.O. BOX 635
LYNNWOOD, WA 98046

Once, something in America was
    simply just not right:
white people owned black people, so
    the states began to fight.

The north states fought the southern states
    to set black people free.
As war raged on, a baby boy
    was born in slavery.

This boy, George Carver, lived deep in
    Missouri on a farm.
He lost his mother during war
    but God kept him from harm.

The Civil War came to an end
    in eighteen sixty-five,
and little George was free and as
    he grew began to thrive.

He walked the woods, where he observed
    God's wonderful creation—
new plants and bugs and animals—
    with endless fascination.

He was so good with nature that
    his neighbors and his friends
would bring sick plants to him to nurse
    them back to health again.

He had so many questions about
        insects, plants, and weeds,
and knew the way to find the answers
        was to learn to read.

So George, at age eleven, waved
        a final, sad goodbye
to all the friends whom he would miss.
        He set his sights sky-high.

He walked toward a poor black school—
        eight lonely, dusty miles—
and stopped along the way to study
        plants a little while.

He practiced talking, for he felt
        self-conscious when he spoke;
a cough when young made his voice high
        and squeaky in his throat.

He heard a school bell and felt very
        shy as he arrived.
A girl yelled out, "You comin' or not?"
        George—nervous—stepped inside.

He sat right up in front because
　　of reading skills he lacked,
but learned so fast by lunch the teacher
　　moved him farther back.

He did chores at a family's home
　　to earn a place to stay.
They gave him his own Bible that
　　he learned to read each day.

And though the Bible answered questions
　　George had about God,
he still had questions about nature
　　other books could solve.

So after two years, when he'd learned
        more than his teacher knew,
he traveled west to Kansas to
        attend a black high school.

George loved the school but then one day—
        before he graduated—
two white men stopped him as he walked.
        He clutched his books and waited.

One sneered, "No black boy can read books.
        They're stolen books, aren't they?"
George said, "They are my schoolbooks, sir,"
        then tried to back away.

The man grabbed George and punched him in
        the stomach with his fist.
George doubled over in a ball
        and tried hard to resist.

He felt a hard boot slam into
    his neck and then his side.
The people who were passing by
    ignored his urgent cries.

The two men laughed, then grabbed his books
    and swaggered down the street.
Without his books, George could not learn.
    His future now seemed bleak.

George had no money to replace
    his precious books and knew
he'd have to quit the school he loved
    and find some work to do.

Four years passed by; then in the year
    of eighteen eighty-three
George graduated, finally,
    with his high school degree.

He took a train to college—
    delighted to be there.
An older woman met him with
    a most unfriendly glare.

"Wait here," she snapped when George told her
    he'd been accepted there.
The principal—red-faced—appeared.
    "I never was aware
that you were of the Negro race.
    We don't take Negroes here."
George silently walked out the door,
    his vision blurred by tears.

Six years went by before George heard
        about another place—
a college that he could attend
        regardless of his race.

The college was in Iowa
        and George was taken in.
They did not seem at first to care
        about a person's skin.

Most students lived in houses, but
        George was assigned a shack
located near the edge of campus,
        in the very back.

George gladly cleaned the spider webs
        and scrubbed the dirty floor.
He could not wait to start his classes,
        study, and explore.

George soon became quite popular
     and also proved to be
one of the brightest students there.
     His class and faculty
were soon embarrassed that he lived
     in such a run-down space,
so they brought blankets, chairs, a bed,
     to furnish George's place.

The students secretly slipped dollar
     bills under his door.
These gifts touched George and made him feel
     accepted even more.

George heard about a college, though,
    much bigger than his own,
where they taught horticulture—all
    about how things are grown,
and how to get the best new crops
    and help make fertile soil,
so food like vegetables and fruit
    would flourish and not spoil.

So George thought, *I could study plants*
    and nature even more
and then help farmers—white and black—
    who are so very poor.

George left the college that he loved
    to go to Iowa State,
from where he was the first black man
    to ever graduate.

He joined Tuskegee Institute—
    a school to teach ex-slaves
how they could farm and grow things well
    and earn a decent wage.

Because the price that cotton farmers
        got was much too low,
George tried to get them thinking of
        another crop to grow—
like good, nutritious peanuts they
        could sell and store and eat.
But—like their parents—they kept planting
        cotton in the heat.

George felt so very frustrated.
        Then in the wintertime
a small and grayish beetle helped
        to change the farmers' minds.

When eggs were laid inside the cotton
        plant by this boll weevil,
they hatched by many thousands and
        began, these tiny beetles,
to eat their way right through the farmers'
        precious cotton crops.
And no one knew of any way
        to make these insects stop.

And so in nineteen hundred four,
    because of this new threat,
George got the farmers planting peanuts—
    a much safer bet.

It was a good idea, since
    the peanut crops grew well,
but people there weren't used to eating
    them. They did not sell.

The merchants would not buy them, so
    the farmers—mad at George—
yelled, "We can only eat a few.
    What good are thousands more?"

So as George took his morning walks,
    he prayed to his Creator,
"What did You make the peanut for?
    Please be my educator."

George sensed that God would show him, and
  he felt quite confident.
He walked back to his laboratory
  to experiment.

He took some peanuts and he broke
  them into little parts
and placed the different elements—
  amino acid, starch,
sugar, pectos, oil, fat,
  and also gum and water—
in beakers, and then mixed and made
  some cooler and some hotter.

The different temperatures and different
  pressures that George used
on all these elements created
  products that were new.

George worked so steadily that by
    the end of the third day,
he let his students in to see
    the wonderful display
of products made from peanuts no
    one else had thought to do,
like ink and milk and facial cream
    and even some shampoo.

George said, "God, our Creator, has
    a use for everything.
We must discover what that is
    and use our reasoning."

He went to share his knowledge with
    important businessmen.
He climbed the steps to City Hall.
    Before he could walk in,
the doorman yelled, "Hey, not so fast!"
    and kicked at George's case.
"Get out! We do not need the likes
    of you in this fine place."

George showed his invitation, yet
    because his skin was black,
he had to go around to enter
    from the very back.

George stepped into the meeting, glad
to be with friends again,
but also sad that some look down
on people with dark skin.

The men were awed at all the peanut
products George presented:
new cereals, fruit punch, coffee, and
the dyes that he'd invented.

George soon was known throughout the States
    as "Mr. Peanut Man."
The farmers started living well
    on their productive land.

Increasingly George gained respect
    from black people and white,
the northerner and southerner,
    the rich and poor alike.

And Thomas Edison, another
    great inventor then,
was so impressed he asked George if
    he'd come to work for him.

He offered George a well-equipped
        and splendid laboratory
and also, for that time, a most
        enormous salary.

George turned this offer down and others
        that soon came his way.
He loved to teach and help the poor,
        which filled up all his days.

When George was sixty-four years old,
        he felt quite pleased to be
awarded with an honorary
        doctorate degree.

George Carver—great inventor—died
    in nineteen forty-three.
He'd used the talents God gave him,
    and so creatively.

He overcame great prejudice
    and used his brilliant mind
to study God's creation and
    to truly bless mankind.

Like George, who kept on searching for
    inventive ways to give,
we too must use the gifts we have
    to bless those where we live.

Christian Heroes: Then & Now

by Janet and Geoff Benge

Heroes for Young Readers and Heroes of History for Young Readers are based on the Christian Heroes: Then & Now and Heroes of History biographies by Janet and Geoff Benge. Don't miss out on these exciting, true adventures for ages ten and up!

Continued on the next page...

Heroes of History

by Janet and Geoff Benge

Abraham Lincoln: A New Birth of Freedom
Benjamin Franklin: Live Wire
Christopher Columbus: Across the Ocean Sea
Clara Barton: Courage under Fire
Daniel Boone: Frontiersman
Douglas MacArthur: What Greater Honor
George Washington Carver: From Slave to Scientist
George Washington: True Patriot
Harriet Tubman: Freedombound
John Adams: Independence Forever
John Smith: A Foothold in the New World
Laura Ingalls Wilder: A Storybook Life
Meriwether Lewis: Off the Edge of the Map
Orville Wright: The Flyer
Theodore Roosevelt: An American Original
William Penn: Liberty and Justice for All

…and more coming soon. Unit study curriculum guides are also available.

Heroes for Young Readers Activity Guides
Educational and Character-Building Lessons for Children

by Renee Taft Meloche

Heroes for Young Readers Activity Guide for Books 1–4
Gladys Aylward, Eric Liddell, Nate Saint, George Müller

Heroes for Young Readers Activity Guide for Books 5–8
Amy Carmichael, Corrie ten Boom, Mary Slessor, William Carey

Heroes for Young Readers Activity Guide for Books 9–12
Betty Greene, David Livingstone, Adoniram Judson, Hudson Taylor

Heroes for Young Readers Activity Guide for Books 13–16
Jim Elliot, Cameron Townsend, Jonathan Goforth, Lottie Moon

…and more coming soon.

Designed to accompany the vibrant Heroes for Young Readers books, these fun-filled activity guides lead young children through a variety of character-building and educational activities. Pick and choose from the activities or follow the included thirteen-week syllabus. An audio CD with book readings, songs, and fun activity tracks is available for each Activity Guide.

For a free catalog of books and materials contact
YWAM Publishing, P.O. Box 55787, Seattle, WA 98155
1-800-922-2143, www.ywampublishing.com